AYG?

Stories never told before

Lehlohonolo Mchunu

I wrote this for my great grandmother

We are best friends, you taught me a lot about life that most parents would not easily share with their children, you spoke openly about almost everything I'd question and not question. You raised me like a direct seed of absent womb, you bathed me, clothed me, accompanied me to crèche and sent me to school, you knew my troubles even before I could share them, in my teens you treated me like a gentleman, I matured earlier than most my peers, your treatment towards me would seem like it was harsh, only now I see that you were grooming me for independence and greatness. You did not give me laws to live by, you injected virtues within me. And that's what I needed most to come out of most challenges I faced. Some, if not most of what I discuss in this book are the only things I couldn't tell you face to face. I've always been a writer and that's the best way I know how to pour out my heart.

And to my mother,

I thank you firstly for enduring the months of physical changes to your body carrying me in your womb. You were young and had two choices, to terminate the pregnancy or keep it, and you were bold enough to keep the pregnancy for its full duration until I was born. After birth you could have thrown me away but, regardless the conflicts you had within you, you stood firm for me in the end. Secondly, I thank you for believing in me no matter what, we had our own struggles and still you never stood in the way of my dreams and aspirations, you are a star.

To my grandmother,

Ours is a story for another day, we spent our time together as tourists, when we speak of hustlers, I think of you. You stepped in, a streetwise lady from Soweto, Zola. My stay in Soweto was overseen by you and you made sure that Soweto does not swallow me whole.

To my family,

My late grandfather, JP Chua and his late older brother, TS Rammupudu I was a little trouble they didn't want while working because work would be cut short by my unending questions and comments. To the remaining brother of my grandfather, JT Rammupudu, we speak a lot about politics lately but, I'm forever inspired by your achievements to be better and do greater, and to your wife (T Rammupudu), I've found a second mother and not a grandmother, she's very young (in spirit) to be seen as grandma. To your sons and daughter, Tshidiso, Kgaogelo and Albertina I've found siblings who always awake my potential in sharpening my brains.

And to my relatives and neighbours in the village of Tafelkop, Limpopo province.

Thank you for being such amazing people, I've never felt afraid walking through the night in our village because, I always knew that I am home in Tafelkop, thanks for the fruit trees in your yards, they strengthened our bonds. Thanks for the maize fields that would also provide us with numerous vegetables and some wild spinach (Morongo), thank you.

To my school mates,

What can I say? Because we shared so many great memories, the jokes, the debating, the morning rush to finish off home works and assignments. We had fun.

To my pumpkin, well, there are a number of you, but, he knows himself.

Thanks for the great lessons of life. I'm glad we didn't end off on awkward ground, still wishing you all the best in your endeavours.

I wrote this book for you,

My friends, former colleagues, acquaintances and social media friends. And yes, I wrote for you, Sibongile Moyo, Xoliswa Nhlapho, Bongani Zondo, Refilwe Kubyane, my smile keepers and laughter compatriots, while writing this book.

Table of contents

1. Terrors and sea bottom
   The terrible night
   The next morning and days after
   Lunchtime
   A hot slap in the face
   Death where are you?

2. The egg has hatched
   Incubation
   The shell is breaking
   Learning to fly

3. It's a taboo
   Homosexuality
   Now what
   How will we do it?
   Just like that?

4. From bad to worse
   A beast unleashed
   Meeting my Dr
   Do we ever learn?
   A corrupted soul

5. Dead
   Invitation for death
   Not knowing was better than knowing
   Where to, from here?

6. Lost and found
   A day at the park
   Renewed hope
   FYI
   Another visit to the Dr
   The train rides

7. AYG?
   The soccer star and TV personality
   Lost count
   AYG?

   Diction
   Gallery

1. Terrors and sea bottom

The terrible night

I usually took a walk in the evenings after work. I would go to my place from work and change clothes then be out for the walk, the walk was my form of exercise and a way of refreshing my mind.

On that day it was not different, I returned from work and changed my clothes. I wore some cotton workout shorts and short-sleeved t-shirt, then my favourite pair of shoes that were very comfortable and very well made for the walk, I loved them dearly.

I used a different route this time around, it was a little longer and with more streets that had no streetlights on. It was dark but, walkable since there were people still roaming around, as I started going further down the street, it started to get quiet and with less to no movement of people at all. I felt a strong breeze of wind not cold or hot, I was sweating, and my heart rate was very high and wild thoughts seldom hit on me. I took out the earphones and switched off the phone, there was what looked like a bushveld at the curve of the street, I decided to curve with the street and avoid that area which also looked like a dumping site, I also started walking a little faster than I did at first. Few more steps to get out of the dodgy place, two young men grabbed me from behind, I did not resist much as they made it a point to reveal the sharp deadly objects they had. They dragged me to the bushes I was avoiding, there were two more guys there. I was prepared to hand over my phone or anything I had on me, if I can get away from them unharmed. Well, I was in the wrong, they did not want anything from me but, their motive was far from what I anticipated. One of them said;

"Is this him? "

The other responded;

"Yeah, it is him. But, he doesn't really show"

Now, I was perplexed and lost. What do they want from me? My thoughts ran wilder. I was starting to think that, this had something to do with drugs.

"oh, no! This can't be happening" I thought to myself.

Still in this 'no direction argument' one asked me;

"are you Lehlohonolo Mchunu?"

"yeah" I responded

The other spanked my butt, with some 'compliments'

"that's some nice ass you got there. When do you plan to serve it to me, boy?"

At this point my heart was pounding, sweat started flowing like I'm in a shower. He was caressing his hard erected penis with one hand while the other was in my shorts already, it was obvious that I was nervous and would sprint at any time, that was when the other three guys held me to bend over with my head between the legs of one and the other one held my arms while another took down my shorts as the 'chief' was taking down his trousers and lubricating his penis with saliva, he came in behind me as I was facing down, they also tied a cloth around my mouth so I couldn't scream. It was horrible and painful, and when I thought it was done, the second one came in, they all penetrated me right after one had ejaculated and the act continued until I couldn't feel pain, my body was feeble, and I was left there in the dump. Standing up was a struggle, and I still had to walk back home in the night. I felt like I could die right there and then. Down was flowing semen from my anus which was now in excruciating pain. I got to my place, didn't even bath, I just spread out myself on the bed slept facing down.

The next morning and days after

I woke up, my anus was still in pain but, I managed to bath. I turned to the mirror to put on my all time make up that never runs out, my smile. Took my bag and left to catch a train to work. I wanted the train coach of "choirs", gospel songs would put me at ease, at least that's what I thought.

With every twist and turn, my mind would go back to last night's act. I kept a silent lamentation. The train got to New Canada station and I boarded out to get into one going to Westgate station since, this one was going to park Station. While waiting, I thought deeply of what had happened to me. I WAS RAPED! How will I report that to the biased police of South Africa? I shall then die with this within me. Anger built up. I went to work, the day went on like the previous ones, more work, office chats and laughs.

Going back home was yet another pain. I got home and yes, I was going to go for a walk as always but, this time around I got a pocket knife, still new and very sharp. I was ready to kill them, and if they overpower me, I'll die at least having stabbed one of them. I went out and took the same route that I took last night. I didn't see them, the following days too. They were no where to be seen.

One day I was at the mall and guess who I met in the mall's toilets? The "chief" of those guys. He knew me, and I realized who he was, I starred him straight in the eyes. He was trembling and hastily left the toilets, after I was done I found him waiting for me on the benches of the mall, I went over after he "politely" called me over.

"I'm really sorry for what happened the other day"

I looked at him for some time after he uttered those words.

"can you undo it?" I asked

He kept silent

"exactly my point, and what are you apologizing for? Forcing yourself on me? Having your friends stick their penises in me? Leaving me alone in the dump unconscious? Your homophobic comments? What exactly are you apologizing for?"

Now he was even more ashamed or whatever the state you may say to describe his hanging face, his countenance had dropped drastically. I stood up and left.

Later, that day, I got a text from him. I knew he knew me from social media and got my number from there. The text read, "I really am sorry for what happened, and I know that I can't undo the pain I caused you, the thing is I have feelings for you I just love you but, this can't be right since we're both men"

Wait right there, I read the message several times and I couldn't help but, reply.

"raping another man being a man yourself makes it right to fight your sexual orientation insecurities? Imagine if I had opened a case against you for rape, how would that be? There's nothing to be forgiven about in this. Don't you dare text me again"

Well, he kept texting me and I didn't respond to any of his texts, I also blocked his number.

Lunchtime

I had enough money to get myself a nice meal from McDonald's, so, there I was sitting and enjoying my meal when a gentleman came to the table and sat without any invitation.

"hi, you must be Lehlohonolo Mchunu, right"

The last time a stranger called out my name I was raped. I replied;

"no, I'm not the person"

He went through his phone and showed me a picture of myself.

"so, who is he?" he asked

"and who is this supposed to be?" I asked

"you speak exactly like him, sarcastic as well and I like that"

Yes, he was a descent man and somehow, someone I could share the table with.

"I am Lehlohonolo Mchunu" I replied.

He couldn't hide his "excitement" as he smiled and blushed, everyone in the restaurant could see that.

"may I pay for this meal?" he asked.

I showed him the slip and replied,

"I paid already, thank you"

The meal cost something above R60 so, he took out a R100 note saying,

"now I'm paying for it"

I returned it to him in response,

"thanks, but, this one is on me"

He gave me his business card and asked my number, which I gave him. He left me to enjoy my meal. The girls on the next table exclaimed, "sies!" in great irritation and hate.

I finished my meal and left.

A hot slap in the face

There I was, minding my own business on a not so busy street in Braamfontein when I came across a group of guys who also seemed to know me.

"slay queen!" one of them shouted at me as they approached.

"what would a man want in this?" he further asked looking at me in a disgusted face, frowned.

I attempted to just pass by without any comment. Then a very hot slap on the face stopped me. They laughed, and that one guy again said;

"are you that afraid of girls to go for boys? Sies! You're a disgrace!"

Still in silence I rushed out of their sight, they stood there laughing, uttering words of hatred and insults. I never looked back. I wanted to cry but, I wasn't going to allow that to happen. I'm stronger than that, I thought to myself.

This was a second time being attacked, and for what? Being Lehlohonolo Mchunu?

I went to the taxis to get one to return to my place. I decided to go to the mall instead. I don't know what is wrong with me and that mall's toilets. There I was again in the toilet, peeing and was intruded, another slap on the side of my face from behind. What? I turned fixing my trousers.

"you still consider yourself a man? Rubbish! You people should have toilets of your own" a very great statured guy said.

Will I stand to be assaulted again? I left him there with his friends.

Death where are you?

With all the assaults I had faced, I was left with no strength in me to go on. To whom would I turn to for a chat? Everyone seemed to have judged me already and I felt like I'm drowning deeper and deeper into this sea of terror and hatred. My wish was death.

I wanted to die and with no one assisting, I was to commit suicide. There I was, crossing Mandela bridge. I stopped like one who was admiring the work of an engineer who worked the railway lines below, only I knew that I was waiting for the oncoming train that seemed to be at a very great speed to hit one and die instantly but, I was also thinking of the power lines below that I had to encounter once I jump off the bridge, it meant I'd be electrocuted and be roasted before falling on the tracks. Still in my thoughts, my cell rang.

"hi, where are you? I'd love to take you out for lunch"

It was "Mr McDonald's", well, let's just call him, sweet plum. He knew I wasn't working since it was a weekend.

"I'm in Jo'burg"

"OK, can we meet at park Station? Please. "

"alright, I'm going there now"

OK, maybe not today death. At that very moment I rushed to park station and told death to halt a bit.

He called again asking where I was, we met and went to Sandton. We had fun, held hands throughout our strolls, played around like little children at an amusement park, and speaking of an amusement park, we extended to the hours of our meeting and went to gold reef city for the rides. We loved almost the same rides, our adrenalin is a crazy one and very high. For a moment I forgot to ask my compatriot death, where are you? Sweet plum was the only person who knew how to take me away from my miserable thoughts of the terrible assaults.

Death where are you? Stay there for now, I'll see you later.

2. The egg has hatched

Incubation

All animals that lay eggs need to incubate the eggs, so that they develop and are ready to be hatched for the offspring to come out. But, the trick is; they never really know the colour of the offspring that will come out, whether it will look the same as the parents or not. They only do their natural duty of incubating the eggs and the rest will be dealt with in due time.

This happens to humans too, you're pregnant with a baby boy or girl, after birth you raise them according to their gender and expectations towards that particular gender, forgetting that, there are still psychological factors that you have no power to control or change, there is still a spirit within that child that is only controlled by the owner of the brain within that child, which is that child themselves.

Once the shell breaks, expect a whole lot more than what you know. I too, passed through incubation. I Was raised in a way which seemed "right" for me as a child, got toys, books that were meant to assist in my upbringing into whatever was expected of me as a baby boy. As you grow, regardless, the incubation process comes to an end and the shell needs to be broken.

The shell is breaking

Everyone waits in great anticipation when the shell starts to break. At this point parents must step aside and let the young breakout of their shell.

This is where you start saying out the first words, taking the first steps, calling out names, holding a cup on your own to drink, eating your own food with no spoon feeder, interact with other children at school, start making friends and exploring those things that you never discuss at home but, you are expected to know whether they are right or wrong. Your brain starts being challenged to reason without help from parents, growing up to find your identity as an individual apart from family, friends or society at large.

This is a stage where as an individual, find what defines you and on what grounds. This is where decisions are made, to be a follower or trendsetter. And here it's where many fail or succeed in life. Make it or break it. Who are you?

Learning to fly

Then you come to a stage where you need to fly out of the nest. Go now to build your own nest. Now the character of your being runs deeper on either your true self or your deceitful self, this is where you need to live by the choice you took when breaking out of the shell, at this stage you can make a sharp change of route but, you've built relationships and forts already that may be drastically affected by the sharp turns you might take in the air.

3. It's a taboo!

Homosexuality

Indeed we grew up this being a taboo, based on theological law which may also be viewed as natural law and customary law from different regions of Africa and the world, also it may be viewed as a psychological problem or simply spiritual problem (going back to theological law and customary law), and I personally don't dispute any of the above but, we cannot act and treat homosexuality like it doesn't exist. Persecution or discrimination will never resolve "the problem", instead will result in more people being curious and sneaking about at night or from one country to another to satisfy their curiosity.

Yes, we are born male and female species of humans and our reproductive organs are there for the very purpose of reproduction but, for reproduction to take place there are several factors that must come in terms for it to be implemented. Reproduction is a result of two different cells from two different genders of the same species, my view and I stand to be corrected.

Sexual orientation is a result of what comes to an individual based on several factors like social circles, molestation, yes, perhaps demons, in a spiritual perspective and other reasons that can only be found out in an individual's explanation of the desired sexual orientation. Either way, it is happening, and we cannot hide it away or wish it away.

Sexual orientation has had many explanations and subcategories within it. Homosexuality, bisexuality, heterosexuality (which is the "right" form of sexual orientation). That's all I'd focus on for now. As the matter of gender orientation, that is a topic for another day, sorry to my transgender and cisgender friends.

In my understanding of the homosexual, sexual orientation is, someone who finds sexual pleasure in those of the same gender as them either orally or through penetration. A man attracted to men and a woman attracted to women regardless the sexual behavior they prefer, this person will never be able to find sexual pleasure in people of a different sex other than theirs.

Bisexuality, in my understanding it's curiosity, and these never mind having sex with either of the genders in their species. A man who has a wife and still goes out for other men. I can't say a bisexual person is confused because, they know exactly what they are doing. Some only have wives to reproduce offspring as it is "expected" of them by family or society.

Now what?

So, there I was with "sweet plum", a fine gentleman of great stature with dreadlocks that were very long, thin and extremely clean, a well trimmed beard and a fair light skin complexion. When he touched me, my body would be feeble and heat up, adrenalin rushes everywhere. He would always complement my smile and "tall body" which in his complements would say it's "sexy". We became very close friends and we were too comfortable around one another to even be naked in private with no shame.

He would always make me feel like, I am a prince while on the other side he would say I complete his "world", we started having sex after 3 weeks we met, as for kissing, we had already been doing that that from our second meeting.

I never dropped the ball on my rape issue even after he knelt down to engage me for marriage. I wore his ring and not even my family knew that the ring was in actual fact an engagement ring not just an accessory. I was determined to only break the news once we settled a date for our marriage ceremony.

How will we do it?

One night after supper we started discussing our upcoming wedding.

"how would you like our wedding to be like" he asked.

I can tell he was waiting for an answer like one from brides to be. I'm sorry but, my sanity always kicks in too hard on serious questions like this one. After I had sipped my juice and a long but, also short analysis with my mind I responded;

"you'll not be marrying a woman, right? So, there will be no white dress or have your usual wedding ceremony, we're not usual people but, both men who want to simply record their union officially. Our marriage is not recognized theologically or in our African traditions but, the constitution of the Republic of South Africa recognizes our marriage and I'd like us marry not in a magistrates' court, the high court or the appeal court of South Africa but, the constitutional court of South Africa."

I went back to my juice, I could see the perplexity in his eyes, he couldn't hide it. He took my juice to sniff it, checking whether it was infused with an intoxicating substance. And all he said after that was;

"wow!"

We both laughed, and he came back.

"are you serious?"

"which religious leader or traditional leader would contradict their beliefs in our union and conduct our marriage? Let's face reality, only the constitution of this country recognizes us. So, we marry at the court and proceed to our chosen reception, even the constitutional court premises can be used for our wedding ceremony since they also host numerous events there"

"of all that attracted me to you, your intellect surpasses it all" he replied, still in his astonishment.

I was determined to get married at the constitutional court and nothing was ever going to shift my mind from that.

Just like that?

Our lives seemed to be on a good track and at the right pace.

When you value someone, time is nothing, it just passes by unnoticed. We grew to know one another deeper and deeper but, I still did not drop the ball about the rape, and that event would haunt me on other nights while we would attempt to have sex. Sometimes before sleeping I would visit his gin bar, get few sips or gulps of the spirits I would find there. He noticed this change of behavior and attempted asking what was wrong, but, I'd always give lame excuses like, "I've had a rough day at work". We would now have one another's phone without worry because, we were an "item", right?

Several times he'd ask what was wrong with me, especially during sex as I'd snap in the act or be jumpy and have sharp mood turns.

Well, he thought I was cheating, and it became worse when I started distancing myself from him. He started being overly controlling, tracking my trips, calling almost every few minutes, I had to report any changes to my schedule, well, that department of reporting, I'd fail, to this day. Ask my great grandmother or grandmother or even my mother, they will all agree, that I'm failing in the aspect of reporting, I'm just full of surprises. So, failing to report would raise a lot of arguments and being Lehlohonolo Mchunu, also knowing how to answer, our arguments would be the worst challenge of our relationship, and sexually it would depend on my mood and since I'd be pissed almost every time we argue, he wouldn't get some. He got it from someone I knew from social media and I didn't care, I was now in it for the benefits, well, little benefits like lunches, travel to desired destinations, meetings with prominent people for my other aspired careers like journalism, play writing, radio production and others in media as a whole. We grew cold to one another.

The boy he was having sex with somehow recorded their sex session one day and "mistakenly" sent it to me. What a nerve!

During the time I got this sex video of them, "sweet plum" was busy with the preparations for a very huge concert to take place in Jo'burg and I asked him about the boy. He turned it all on me, my mood swings and all. I showed him that video.

"imagine if it went viral? And as for this boy, he is very young, imagine what it'd do to your career"

The event was underway, and I was at the backstage mingling with some unknowns. The next time I saw him at the event, he was with the boy. I went to them, took out the ring and gave it to the boy.

"I think this was meant for you"

I left the event with the chauffeur he got for me. I went to my place and never stepped in his house ever, I left the access cards and all other stuff with the chauffeur to give him. I left him, just like that. Crazy, right?

I wouldn't stand to be assaulted by him every time he felt like less a man and wants to regain respect or whatever he called it. I was never assaulted by my late father and I have no scars of lashes from any of my family members and I wasn't going to stand and give up my body to a stranger to be deformed. I got slaps from him and punches, I wasn't prepared to lose a tooth or break a bone by him. So, yes, I left him. Just like that.

4. From bad to worse

A beast unleashed

We broke up and I soared the skies like a scavenging vulture over the desert. I turned purple of anger and bitterness, all the insults I once got, returned and I was now determined to prove a point and or break hearts, just like mine was broken. I went clubbing, made" friends" with those who had their hearts broken and lived for one reason, that they woke up. Some had lost hope on their dreams and aspirations.

Now I met men for cash, I was a prostitute. We'd meet and agree on these; I offer you anal and oral sex in exchange for cash, some it was only to spite their homophobic girlfriends and others it was only pure pleasure. I was a little beast hungry for sex to clear my mind from past events or then, sex was my only addiction or the only way to keep sanity nearby. It made me feel like I was dominating a certain part of life.

In this soaring of the skies, I got more involved with bisexual men, remember my definition of bisexuality? Yes, they were curious about anal sex and oral sex which they'd tell me that they don't get from their wives or girlfriends.

Some well known media personalities, sports stars, musicians and other "prominent men" in society I received their invitations. I was lose, very lose.

Meeting my doctor

In this sex addiction of mine, I'd use protection with some and others not. So, I woke one morning with an excruciating pain around my anus. And for some unknown reason I took my finger down there, I nearly collapsed after the discovery of an unusual thing.

What's this? I asked myself. I laid on bed, spread my legs and again examined with my finger, it felt like little plant shoots, they were many. I was shaking, but these things are on my body and I need to see this, I took a picture with my phone and immediately after seeing it, the pain vanished and my heart pounded, everything paused for several minutes.

I went to the clinic and had an HIV test, the results were negative, that was a relief. But, another issue now is that growth around my anus, I asked about the health 4 men clinic and they said it was open, I rushed there. This is another part of the clinic that deals with issues related to men who have sex with men, the centres are still few in South Africa and only operate at selected clinics at least this one was nearby.

I met my doctor and I was ready to take his orders and comply without difficulty. He said take off your trouser after seeing the picture I took. I hastily took off my trousers and the underwear, got on the bed and spread wide my legs, he put on the gloves and leaned over, I almost jumped out of the bed when he pocked me. He apologized and laughed a bit.

"someone has been naughty lately" he commented

"yeah, eish!" I shyly responded.

"don't worry, you'll be good in few days, it's just few warts that will disappear. I'll give you something to help"

"warts? don't worry doc, I'll Google it. Don't need more terrifying explanations"

He laughed and said,

"don't forget your trousers on the floor"

We were too comfortable, and I couldn't realize that I'd not put on my trousers yet. So, now I was relieved.

"hloni, take care and please use a condom at all times."

"I will do so, thank you, Dr"

Do we ever learn?

Few days later I was in good state to continue where I left off. I met someone else, and yes, I wasn't prepared to accept any marriage proposal and he understood that very well.

I was seeing other guys on the side whilst with him. We arranged a day to have sex and sex without a condom. That evening came, and I slept over at his house, we had sex and sex and more sex. The following morning, I went to the toilet and again for some unknown reason I wiped myself and looked at the toilet paper.

Blood! I saw blood, and I took another toilet paper this time patting gently and having a look, more blood, I was scared, and I was shivering, I didn't tell him what was going on. He took me home and after he left I rushed to the doctor, again.

"hloni! What did you do this time around?"

"blood, Dr. There was blood and a lot of it"

"let's see, go on the bed"

After checking he laughed and told me to get up.

"there's nothing wrong with you, it's just a small cut. Did it all night or got a bigger machine this time?"

He made me shy a little, so, all the fuss for nothing? The Dr and I made great friends from then on. We'd talk even after his work hours, he became my health mentor. He even introduced me to his psychologist friends and therapists.

A corrupted soul

My perception on men changed, I started seeing them as meat to be devoured. If you looked appeasing to the eye and I set a trap that you wouldn't fight to get out of, you were taken for a ride. I started having targets for myself and 90% of them I'd win over. Business men, tourists, university students and even desired high school boys who had overgrown their age in stature, I'd take over.

I had types and even if you resist I'd use the crocodile's style of hunting, stealth. Or a python's. I never minded if it'd take days or weeks, if you were my type I'd go after you until you fall in my hands on your own accord. I'd use carelessly my natural abilities to manipulate you into doing what I want. I was a walking corpse and I was prepared to shutter other souls with me. The pain I faced had to be faced by someone else and over ten times more. Even those who "genuinely loved" me I was blind to see them. Because I was broken.

5. Dead

Invitation for death again

Death where are you now? I think I'm done. What else do I live for? I'm broken, very broken and not even God would accept me now.

Have you ever been so demotivated that no one makes sense to you when they speak of aspirations, "new beginning" and all that's good. I attempted suicide twice and failed. So, I was just wondering around to see if there would be someone volunteering to kill me, I'd walk around Soweto at any time of night, bypass places that would be declared death traps but, I came out alive.

Death seemed to be on holiday or he also shunned me?

Not knowing was better than knowing

I was brought up in a Christian family, we prayed every morning with my great grandmother, midday and midnight prayers, evening prayers, giving grace before meals, prayers before traveling and prayers upon arrival to our destinations, prayers for heath wellbeing, prayers against evil and on and on. Prayer is a lifestyle to my great grandmother, she never gets in bed in the evenings before praying, even if she may be sick or feel offish, she'd never rest her head before praying.

So, all of this was part of my life and when I stopped living in this manner, I started being fearful and having nightmares. I'd sleep with the lights on, because sometimes I would feel like I was in bed with unknown things. I wished I had never devoted myself to the Christian faith at first. In Christianity we believe in the existence of Heaven and hell, and all the disobedient regardless, go to hell. And here I was disobedient, doing wrong knowing very well that it is wrong, hurting families by making their husbands and or fathers, sons absent instead of spending time with them, yes, the men I had sex with had a responsibility to stick to, however, I cannot say I did not contribute to them shunning their responsibilities. I was at a state of derangeness.

Where to, from here?

I was a lost case, living because, one, the sun rose again and two, I'm not dead yet. The Dr tried getting hold of me and I ignored his calls and even blocked him on social media. I was a machine on auto mode, I took no charge of my life, like a kite, I'd flow to any direction the wind blew me to.

I'd wait for my "friends" to suggest something, then I'd do. I stopped taking decisions completely. What "friends" said, would go. I was dead.

6. Lost and found

A day at the park

Since death denied me, again, I kicked and realized that I was still alive. I got up and switched over to manual mode, it was time I took charge of my life.

I got up one morning, cleaned my room and bathed, got a train to Johannesburg, and went to Braamfontein, chilled at the park near the Jo'burg theatre, and put on my earphones to listen to music and watch the clouds above. Still staring at the sky, a familiar face showed up, he spoke but, I couldn't hear as I had my earphones on. I took them out and sat up straight on the lawn and he joined by sitting next to me.

"and what happened? You just disappeared and no longer took my calls. Are you okay?"

It was the Dr.

"hi, doc. I'm okay, and nothing is wrong with me"

"are you sure, you're okay?"

The Dr knew me a bit more, and he insisted that I talk to him or he'd just stay there with me all day. As if I minded him being there, we stayed and laid on the lawn looking at the sky, forming shapes or creatures with the passing clouds.

Time flew drastically, and it was time to go. He held my hand.

"we stayed here almost the whole day, come let's got grab something to eat. And I'm not taking a 'no' as an answer"

We went to the nearest restaurant open and had a meal. He also drove me home. What a day!

Renewed hope

I was now slow on fishing for men, I was starting to enjoy my time alone with my senses. I'd even started on working on a book that I wrote few years back and gave up since publishers had rejected it. I took advices from other publishers to have the book published and I restarted it from the beginning, it took more and more of my time, I was focused on completing it.

I had the manuscripts in my phone and I'd read it repeatedly whenever I'd find a comfortable place to stay in. While on the book at a restaurant, a gentleman came over to my table.

"this is a picture I don't usually see, a young person like you so focused and drinking an espresso, are you a blogger, Sir?"

My sarcastic self forgot to kick in after seeing his face.

"I'd like to have a blog of my own but, now I'm only reading a manuscript I'm working on" "is it? So, you're a writer but, still you know that you can be a blogger"

"have we met before?" I asked sipping on my espresso.

"oh, sorry, where are my manners?"

He introduced himself and told me that he knew me from social media. That question again. He asked;

"are you Lehlohonolo Mchunu?"

"yes, I'm he."

"finally, we meet, I follow you on Facebook mostly, I'm always intrigued by your posts, your intellect is greater than the age you describe on your profile, were you really born in the year, 1996?"

"yes, I was born in 1996. As for the other comments you stated, I'm honoured."

He took my number and whispered these letters to me as a question.

"AYG?"

I knew what the words meant, considering how he asked.

"I'll text you the answer" I replied leaving the table.

FYI

In this period of regaining my being. I started meeting different people from different backgrounds and all had one thing in common. They knew me from social media. This made me scrutinize every post I'd put on social media, especially on Facebook as this is the platform they knew me from.
One of those people came up to me to challenge my intellect and sanity. He said;

"what do you think of gay guys" he asked the question after hailing insults at the LGBT community.

"FYI, I'm gay myself"

He was taken aback and a bit ashamed, and he said,

"but, how? You don't show"

"you also don't show that you are a homophobe. Anyway, to answer your question. I think they deserve to live, aren't they human too? Do you think it's fair everyone questioning your choices with hatred? We're different as individuals, what makes sense to you may not make sense to another. Do you eat pork?"

"yes" he replied

"do you hate people who don't eat pork"

He was a bit ashamed and quoted Bible verses.

"I'm glad that you quoted the Bible, doesn't the same Bible condemn hatred? So, gay people are going to hell, okay, unfortunately you're accompanying them there and worse, you're the first to fall in because you are rolling out a red carpet in front."

He was pissed and never contacted me ever. I'm sorry had I offended you, my friend.

Another visit to the Dr

Immediately after saying come in, he stood up and commented.

"wow! Hloni, you look different today, wait let me guess. You found a man?"

"unfortunately, your guess is incorrect. Try again"

"I don't know but, that smile is genuine, and I want to know where it comes from. Come on, tell me. What's going on?"

"I'm simply, happy Dr. I've come to accept myself and be me and no one else but, me. Either alone or with someone else, I've decided to take charge of my life"

Of course, that was after weeks spent with his psychologist friend and therapist.

"I'm impressed, so how about we go grab a snack?"

"if it's on you, I'd never say no"

"I don't mind, as long as you keep that smile on your face"

We went for the 'kasi food', Kota, simply a quarter of bread filled with several delicacies like, fries, polony, egg, russian, burger, some add atchaar and lettuce, cheese and vianna and on and on. Given that Kota is my addiction, I had a marvellous day.
We went back to the office, so I'd fetch my bag to go back to my place,

"come on, you're leaving? Please wait few minutes, I'm knocking off anyway and I'll drop you off at your place"

It's not like I had a lot to do at my place, so I waited for him to finish up whatever he wanted to do, and we left.

"you're an amazing guy, you know?"

I was blushing, and I reckon my dark complexion self was pale or turning pink to his words.

"is it? Thanks, anyway"

"I somehow, like you man"

"thanks doc. But, I'm gladly single and want to be so."

He looked dull after hearing my response, but we managed to make great friends though, he's happily engaged to the love of his life today, great! Isn't it?

The train rides

For some time, I'd travel to and from work by train and had made some "friends" there. I'd go to the choir coach and felt like the ride would go on and on without stopping, given that I had 'stress' and an 'unstable' sanity. The singing and dancing and clapping would do me good for some time.

On one occasion in the train I saw a guy. He was different in a way, chilled character and very cool if I may say. It wasn't the first time or last time seeing him, I'd see him in the mornings and board in the same coach, sometimes, even in the evenings I'd see him.

He seemed like someone I'd befriend, but, he was also good to be observed from a distance. If I didn't see him I'd be a bit troubled. We never spoke before or ever, we only had silent uncertain conversations from just looking at one another without any fear of doing so. He was the reason I'd enthusiastically want to ride in the train every morning.

7. AYG?

The soccer star and TV personality

There I was, minding my own business and acting like I didn't recognize who he was while everyone around yearned to take a selfie with him. He's always been my crush and today I had to make sure he picks that up but, I don't have to act vulnerable before him.

We went into the same cinema room, his seat wasn't far from mine on the same row, there were two seats between us and they were empty. I gave him an eye, so did he. I couldn't hold it any longer I went over to him.

"hi, sir. May I sit here?"

The smile on his face was enough answer to my question and I sat down before he could respond.

"what if I said no?" he asked

"then, I guess I should leave"

I was about to leave when he pleaded that I should stay.

"you look familiar, are you a member of parliament?" I asked sarcastically.

"wow! Parliament? Definitely not one. Maybe if you tried sports"

"I only love volleyball and I haven't seen you there"

"don't you watch soccer?"

"I'm not a fan, the players, well, some seem decent but, the sport. I really don't like"

He laughed softly, and gave me a look of hunger, he looked like he'd devour me any moment from then.

He introduced himself, and yes, he was a soccer player, well known. Then, I was all the more sarcastic and he liked it. Seconds before the movie started he whispered,

"please, let's chat some more after the movie, if you don't mind"

I smiled "ok" and turned to the screen.

During the movie, he'd place his hand on mine on the armrest, and my response was "positive", we ended up in an interlocked fingers position like lovers strolling in the park, our hands got a bit sweaty. That's how tightened our hands were.

As agreed, after the movie we chat and ended up in his car. We were going to grab a snack on one of his favourite restaurants somewhere north of Johannesburg. We grabbed a snack and later he requested a ride for me to go back to my place as he had to go to camp, or whatever they call it, for training. He had my number and almost every evening he'd call to "check up" on me. We grew very close to one another.

One afternoon having lunch, I was approached by a man, a well-known man.

"are you all by yourself?"

I looked up to see who it was, and I almost screamed but, the little devil within said "sit still and act up like an owner of a conglomerate, act like you don't know who he is". I knew exactly who he was and acted like an alien when he introduced himself to me.

"sorry, I am… (of course I won't mention his name) and I have been observing you from a distance and I must say that I am taken aback by your conduct, mind I join you?"

"to your first question, yes, I'm all by myself. And to your last question, unfortunately, I'm done with my meal and was about to leave. Sorry"

"may I then, have your number?"

"really? I believe the restaurant is filled with people who'd love dearly to provide you with their numbers"

"unfortunately, I want yours"

I asked the waiter for a pen, it was a gel ink pen, my favourite type of pen, then I took a serviette and wrote my number diagonally from the bottom left corner to the top right corner and gave him as I stood up to leave.

Now I'd given a well-known TV personality my contact number, few ladies went on to take selfies with him in enthusiasm while I walked out like a "boss", few other patrons looked at me with perplexity or whatever thoughts they had.

Now, I had two well known guys in my hands or they had me in theirs. Later on, I got a call,

"are you home safe?"

The voice was familiar, and sarcastically I replied,

"aren't you supposed to be in front of the camera? Your show is about to start"

"I'm in the changing room getting ready and thought I should check up on my nutshell friend"

"nutshell? I know that I can be difficult at times but, a nutshell? Please. Yes, I am home and waiting for you to start the show, I'm a huge fan"

"don't stress, I can rehost the show in private and in 5D for you"

"thanks, but, I'm still good with 3D, chat later"

I had him where I always wanted him to be. On one weekend, my soccer star had a match to attend, he knew I was no soccer fan, so, he invited me over to his house the following day. On that match day, I met with my TV star for our first date. We spent the day with his friends going from one club to another, and ended up alone with him in his house, I still don't know how we dodged his friends to end up in his house, and another party started, a party for two. We messed up the house, from the lounge to the bedroom, from the garden to the balcony, we toured the whole house until I couldn't walk anymore. We woke up naked in one of the guest rooms, bottles of alcoholic beverages everywhere, and sachets of his powders. We took a bath and cleaned up the mess, so much for a first date?

Yes, leaving his house I went to my soccer star's house, all cleaned up and hung over. He could tell I'd been up all night.

"someone's been naughty last night?"

"and what will you do about it?"

He loved it when I gave him dominion over me. Do you still want me to tell you what happened after our 5 seconds conversation? Yes, I had more and more sex until the evening of that day, I slept over. The following day was work, he lent me some of his clothes, thanks to my "gigantic" body, I fit in most of his clothes, after getting something convenient, I went to work.

My relationship with both guys was solely for sex, and I had to leave them because, both were starting to get attached and opting a serious relationship, and I really have a problem with well known public figures, so, I had to cut ties with them.

Lost count

I can't deny it, I lost my virginity at a young age through interacting in sexual activities with older than I guys. Yes, there were years of "innocence", years of good behavior, years of being a "good" boy. In those years I had interacted in sex with about 5 guys, at least. Then when I derailed from those years, I was now having sex almost every single day with different men. On one occasion I slept over at one guy's house and the next morning I went to another, and later that day met another. I had at some point counted 6 men in a period of 3 days and a record of 35 men in 6 months. The day I went for a full body check up to the Dr I also opted to take an HIV test, when we got to the HIV test, the Dr asked,

"if the results came out positive, who would you say infected you? And how are going to tell your family?"

I remember sitting back on the chair, a little sigh and coughing a deceitful laugh.

"my family? I won't tell them. And as for, who I'd say had infected me? It'd be any of the 40 guys or more I had sex with"

I remember very well the Dr going dead silent, Jaws dropped and staring at me in great perplexity.

"what?"

That was a first time seeing the Dr run out of words. We did the test. Truly speaking, I was shaking in my pants and almost wet my pants as the results came through. Well, at least I got off this one easily. The results were negative but, if they came out positive, I was prepared to take responsibility for my carelessness and start on the treatment.

So, until the day I started writing this book, I tried counting the men I had sex with, and I lost count at about 101 men, it could be a miscalculation, maybe they are less than 100 or more than that. Celebrities, noble men, husbands, boyfriends, sons, uncles, brothers, nephews, athletes, grandpas and others, so, it could be. I just lost count.

AYG?

Remember the guy in the restaurant who asked, AYG?

I did text him later that day to answer, and my answer was, "yes".

AYG? Was my question to many after being asked the very same question as well. And hence, I lost count of my sex partners, all I asked, replied, "yes"

After replying the guy, he asked me out and I never resisted.

"I really like you"

He said thus when we met and were relaxed in the restaurant of his choice.

"is it?"

In my mind, I had already taken off his shirt and thinking to myself, "he must be beside his sanity, I only do hookups, not this like or love games". I was only rushing to have him all night long. Well, we had a very long conversation but, it was closed by some hot steamy session of lust and all.

Now my answer was, "yes" every time asked, AYG (Are You Gay)? A three letter by three words question whose answer was a three-letter word.

I stop here. A lot happened, and some are so intense in such a way that they can't be shared publicly as they lack alternatives to represent them or lessen their harshness and inhumaneness.

Whatever your perception towards me after reading this, just know my thoughts and perspective towards you are pure and of genuine love.

Diction

Sies! - a verbal expression of being disgusted

Eish! – a verbal expression of uncertainty

Kasi – township

Kota – quarter of bread filled with fries, viannas, eggs, burger, atchaar, and other meaty or dairy products like cheese

Atchaar – salad made of spiced unripe mango fruit downed in vegetable oil, at times chilli and or garlic is added

Gallery

I have attached some photos reflecting my journey in the writing of this book, when you look carefully on them, you will see that the body says nothing bad. It doesn't say I'm sick, it doesn't say I'm hungry or thirsty. By simply looking at these pictures you find nothing wrong, well, except that I'm not in my clothes.

These pictures are exactly what made me get up and dust myself off the negativity and perceptions from people negative towards me and carry myself back in the journey of life. I'd be naked at times and observe my body, and I found out, it has nothing to show that I was raped, and I was not going to drown myself in those events and even halt my dreams because I was raped.

The pictures always motivate me to go on, my eyes still can see, my ears can still hear, my nose and nostrils are still here and functioning well, I can still speak, my hands, limbs and legs and feet are still here and functioning properly, why now give up on life?

That's how I returned.

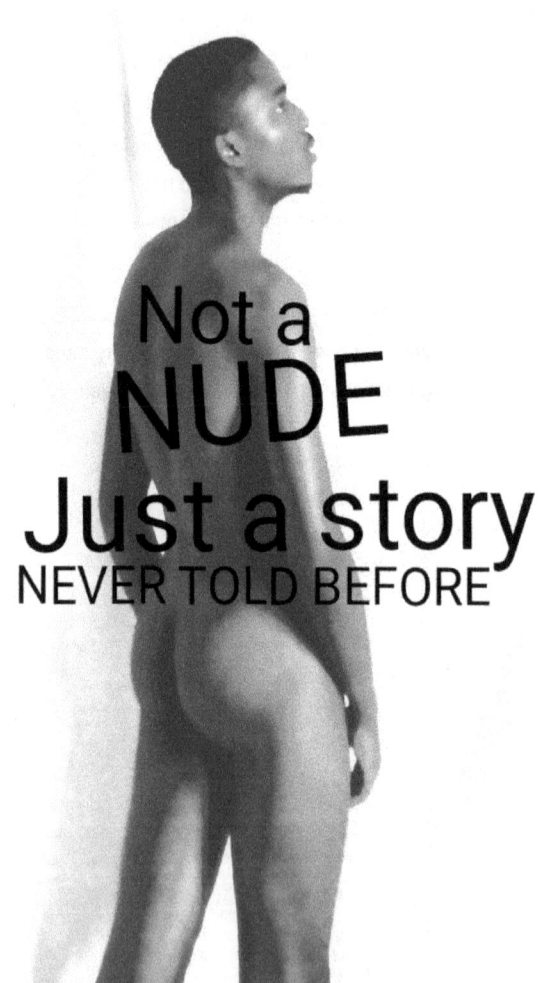

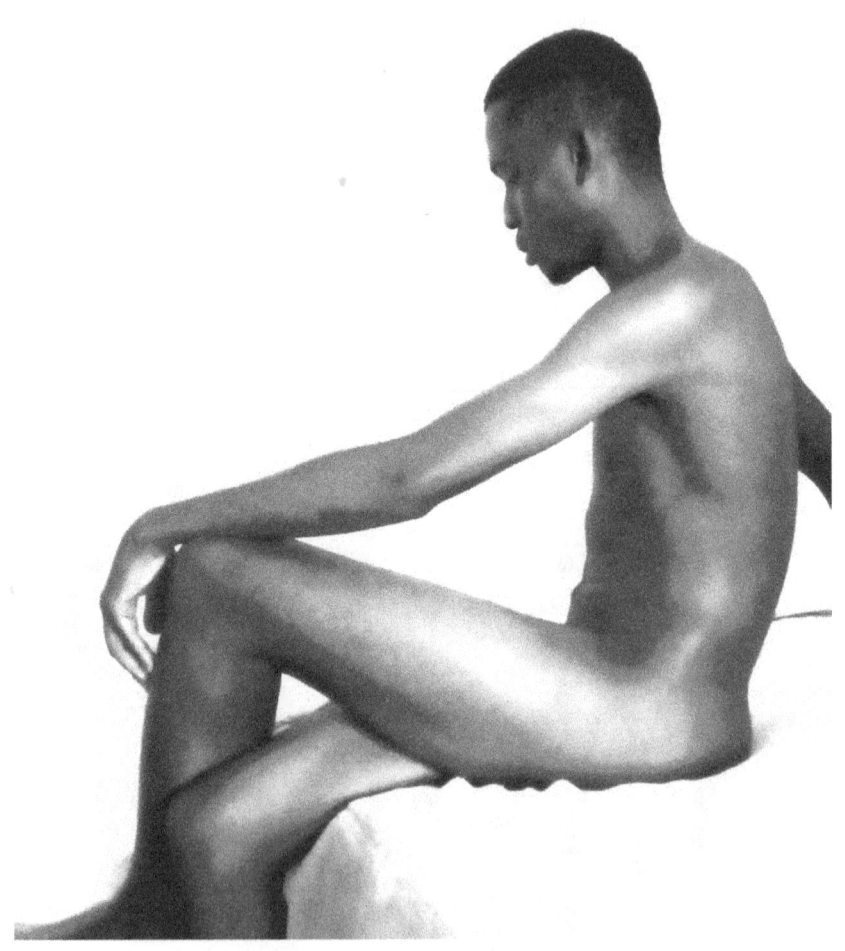

www.ingramcontent.com/pod-product-compliance
Lightning Source LLC
Chambersburg PA
CBHW061300040426
42444CB00010B/2447